C.H.A.R.G.E.

A Young Woman's Guide for Healthy Relationships

A love letter to my granddaughter

STEVE FITZHUGH

Look for Steve's other books on Amazon, Barnes and Noble, or order directly through the author.
www.PowerMoves.org

Cover photo of Steve and Camille
by Siona Fitzhugh

Author photo (page 29)
by John Williams

Edited/Formatted by Kimberly Soesbee
www.KimberlySoesbee.com

Published by Touch Publishing
www.TouchPublishingServices.com

DEDICATION

My world changed September 10, 2016. Camille Eva Fitzhugh arrived, slightly premature, but otherwise healthy and full of life and purpose.

I was smitten! My first grandchild. From the time of her arrival, I was confronted with a stark reality. At my age chances are I may not be around when she reaches her full potential. As much as I'd like to see her graduate, see her walk down the aisle headed to holy matrimony, bounce her kids on my knee, I am aware that these experiences I may or may not enjoy.

At some point in her life, the only things she'll know of me are the memories that we've built before my departure. She'll hear stories about me, perhaps hear some of my sermons, read some of my books, and hear the testimony of the legacy I've left behind. That's life. Her arrival made the light at the end of the tunnel more prominent in my mind than the sound of the gun at the start of my race of life.

I dedicate this book to Camille, in honor of my big sister Greta. Greta died in her prime, and while on her sick bed, she was calling out the name of her first love. He stole her heart at 17 and crushed it beyond repair. Her self-esteem spiraled downward, and she began a life of poor choices in men thinking that was all she deserved. It's too late for Greta. My hope and prayer is that Camille won't experience the heartache like Greta and so many young women do as a result of their poor choices in relationships as they search for love.

I have much to say to young men, but that's for another work. Charge is a brief message/guide for young women. Set your standards high, guard your heart, and seek first the kingdom of God, and all good things will be added unto you.

I love you, Camille, and although you are too young to read this at its publication, one day I pray you would know intimately what it means to be cherished, honored, adored, and respected, because you are truly God's expression.

I love you!
Love, Pop-pop

CONTENTS

WHY C.H.A.R.G.E.?

I will never forget standing in the ballroom of a major downtown hotel in Dallas, Texas. I had just finished my keynote address at a National Youth Convention to over 4,000 youth delegates from throughout the country. As I stood there shaking hands, signing bibles, and answering questions, I noticed one young girl standing off to the side, noticeably waiting to be the last person to have an audience with me. At long last it was her turn. I greeted her and this was her response.

"Mr. Fitzhugh," she began soberly, "I've never had anyone tell me I was pretty or special. The first boy that came along and said the right things, I fell for him. That led me into a pretty bad relationship. I knew he wasn't the right one for me, but I thought I was in love. I'd won a college basketball scholarship to a school in California. After my first season, in my first year, I missed that boy so much that I quit the team, gave up my scholarship, and moved back home. I quickly found out that while I was away, he had been fooling around with two of my best friends. The moment I got home we fooled around too, and he gave me a disease. It's something I have to live with for the rest of my life." She broke down in tears.

My heart sank. Who can fathom the needless heartache, the emptiness, the volumes of shattered lives lying in the wake of the selfish offender who tramples the hearts of the lonely and desperate? We can never overvalue the empirical need to be esteemed and to have self-confidence because it's our self-esteem that thwarts veiled attempts to conquer us, dominate us, use us. Yet this one scene, the young heart starving for approval and applause succumbed by the aggressive hormone-driven adolescent boy, is repeated often throughout America with the same or similar results school year after school year. I have heard this tale so many times I could probably finish the sentences of the next one telling it with some degree of accuracy. My heart breaks every time I encounter such a plight.

Perhaps I am hypersensitive because I am raising two daughters of my own. Perhaps my sensitivity is because as the "baby of the family" I was a "momma's boy." I was a firsthand witness to Mom's victimization: verbal, emotional and physical. I was there, seeing her attempt to pick up the pieces of a failed marriage and struggle to raise four children on her own. Or perhaps my sensitivity is the result of seeing my own sister struggle for acceptance and latch on to men beneath her because her self-esteem was too low to expect anything or anyone better. I have vowed to ensure that my daughters will never have to wonder if they are pretty enough, good enough, or special. As often as possible throughout their lives, I intentionally affirm them. As often as possible, I attempt to demonstrate how they ought to be treated because they deserve it, every time. I often look deeply into their eyes, almost touching their souls when I declare with confidence, "You are so beautiful!"

Because of my work and travels I meet so many who, like my young friend in Dallas, never hear such things. Consequently, when the first "wrong thing" comes along and says the right things, bad things soon happen.

I searched for effective ways to address this phenomenon. I have the privilege of standing before thousands of teenage girls and boys in America who will at some time find themselves in the valley of decision when it comes to relationships. What can I say that will make a difference? When did women become the enemy?

The "final straw" came during a presentation in Springfield, Illinois. On occasion I'll randomly shake hands with a young man and with all seriousness ask, "How's your wife?" Their immediate response is often hilarious. To the girl I'll ask, "How's your husband?"

However, in this instance the young lady responded, "How did you know I had a husband?" She went on to say, "I am graduating in two weeks. I have a husband, but I am not married. I have been seeing a married man now for two years. He promised me he was going to leave his wife and five kids for me. I just found out I am a month and a half pregnant, now he says he doesn't ever want to see me again…what do I do?"

Instances like these drove me to develop the young woman's Power Phrase!

I call it: C.H.A.R.G.E.

When I am in assemblies or giving presentations throughout America, more teens approach me after the show to hear this phrase once again and write it down over any other thing I say. It is a positive profession that establishes what behavior will be accepted and at the same time, what will not be accepted.

This is how I present it:

"Hey ladies! Whoever that guy is…and you know who I'm talking about, don't you…the one that's trying to hang with you…not just anybody, but HIM…make sure he understands the meaning of CHARGE! **C-H-A-R-G-E…tell him…Cherish Me, Honor Me, Adore Me, Respect Me, for I am God's Expression!** If he can't roll like that…he's not the one!"

Negative peer pressure and more importantly, bad peer influence, force students into negative behavior all the time. True champions let the air out of this type of pressure by having a positive self-image of who they are. Without such a self-image, students attempt to find identity by fitting in or going with the flow. I have discovered that any "dead fish" can go with the flow. I can take a dead fish, toss it in the river, and it will take off downstream. I can exhort it to go, go, go when actually it's dead. Why is it moving? It's just caught in the current and going with the flow. The student who can act like, dress like, drink like, smoke like, or cuss like everyone else does not impress me. Anyone can do that! The true champions in life are those who have the courage to go against the flow, even when everyone else is going a different direction. A positive self-confession about who you are is one of the most powerful ways to stand against behavior or treatment that is contrary to who you believe yourself to be. Positive self-confession triggers confidence, character, and courage.

My dear young lady, inherent in your existence is the right and expected end that you are to be CHERISHED, HONORED, ADORED, AND RESPECTED! You are GOD'S EXPRESSION!

The next few pages will detail for you what such an experience should look like, sound like, and feel like. Once you complete this short reading and understand the height, depth, and breadth of who you are and what you deserve, never allow him, no matter who "he" is, to force you to lower your standards just so that he can raise his!

Apply this Power Phrase not only to your relationships but apply it throughout your personal or professional encounters. If you tolerate the contrary, injury is certain, and you will never be fulfilled.

And that which you tolerate you can never change!

C

CHERISH ME

cher·ish   transitive verb /ˈCHerəSH/

- to feel or show great love for (someone or something)
- to remember or hold (an idea, belief, etc.) in a deeply felt way

    Culture can be a crude teacher of expected norms and attitudes. Trends and expectations for interpersonal behavior find their way into our belief system through news media, the entertainment industry, and even social media without us ever putting forth an effort to learn. With teenagers today, what is accepted too often is only what is trending. If we listen closely to the music, women are often casually demeaned; that which at one time was grossly offensive has now become a term of endearment. To **cherish** is something altogether different.

    When you cherish, there is no grey area of

misunderstanding or ambiguous meaning. There is no double entendre or inconspicuous connotation. To cherish is to show great love for someone. It will be evident in how you are spoken to and spoken of. It will be clearly evident in how you are treated and cared for. He will go out of his way to accommodate your pleasure, preference, and completeness. He will make great sacrifices just for your smile. And your smile is the only "thank you" he needs. His words will be choice words, not casual words, when describing how he feels about you because he knows his words need to make you feel special.

The important things in your life that may seem small to others will be huge to him. Anything that's important enough to occupy space in your heart or time on your mind will hold great value to him, for they are the keys to your contentment and fulfillment. He will handle those things with care.

To cherish you is to know you so deeply that he can begin to anticipate what you want, surprise you with it before you ask, and time its arrival that you receive it when you need it most. If he cherishes you, you will see him find joy in simply holding your hand or drinking in your laughter and being satisfied without an expectation of anything more, just because you are you.

When you speak, he will try to capture the intent of your every thought from your every sentence of your every word not only because what you are saying has meaning, but because to him your voice is like magic and hearing you speak is always a thrill. Because he cherishes you, he will drape insignificance over every distraction that might attempt to rob from him the special moments you spend together. He realizes life is short and time is a priceless commodity that cannot be stored, so he refuses to allow his time with you to be dashed by interruptions or diminished by a text, tweet, or phone call that can easily be handled later. He will struggle with every goodbye, welcome every hello, and be committed to celebrate the highs, comfort you through the lows, and work to solve the difficulties in between.

Say it once, "Cherish me."

Say it again out loud, "Cherish me!"

You deserve to be cherished. If this is not your experience, understand one simple principle: You can never get the steak you deserve until you kick all the hotdogs out of your life!

H

HONOR ME

hon·or   noun /ˈä-nər/

- respect that is given to someone who is admired

It is easy to identify those who honor you. **Honor** is directly related to how you are valued and admired. Those who honor you place such high value on who you are that their admiration of you speaks loudly and is demonstrated in how you are treated. When you are honored, you will feel like royalty whenever that person shows up. They recognize the weight of your opinions; they value your wishes and defend you when either of these are threatened.

I have been in the company of couples when the woman is dishonored. I've heard him tell her, "shut up" or call her "stupid" or "dumb." The scars such dishonor leaves behind continue to insult you long after the words have been spoken. Self-opinion erodes, confidence becomes extinguished, while the groundwork for a heart subject to manipulation is established. Desperate for love, she fails to see his dishonorable words are only tools for the master manipulator who needs to dishonor her so that he can feel better about himself. Such dysfunctional relationships show up in society all the time. It is so sad to see toxic people contaminate a healthy heart full of potential, in the name of love. Soon after the infatuation wears off and the break up is done, she is left so wounded she's incapable of fully trusting the next man who comes along.

To be honored is the standard that protects the heart. An easy sign that hurt is close is when his dishonoring of you is frequent, careless, and without remorse. When this is evident, decisions must be made. For pain and suffering will happen in life, but misery is an option. It is one thing in life to experience the everyday typical regrets, but to live in constant misery because of the dishonor you accommodate is something quite different.

Remember, that which you accommodate you will never be able to change. Honor respects and reveres. Honor admires. Honor values. Honor lifts up, but never puts down. Honor does not disappoint. Dishonor shames, blames, ridicules, and belittles. Know the difference; take the high road every time.

Choose honor, choose life, for though you were born to win, you must choose to be a winner.

A

ADORE ME

a·dore   transitive verb /ə-ˈdȯr/

- to love or admire (someone) very much

Are you being adored? To adore someone is to demonstrate that you care deeply, admire, or love them. Love shouldn't hurt. You ought to be adored. You deserve to be loved and admired.

Words that assault as insults, even in play, can land as punches that leave bruised hearts and pulverized egos. Adoration is selfless, patient, and kind. To **adore** is to be considerate, sensitive, and empathetic to the one you love. Take an inventory of how you are spoken to: is it adorable? Take an inventory of how you are treated: is it adorable? Take an inventory of the man who professes how deeply he cares: is his manner towards you adorable?

Adore is a verb; it is action. Some spend

years waiting on that so-called special someone to take action and demonstrate ways that they love and adore. Instead, he sits on the fence of non-commitment, unwilling to go forward or back up. Sitting is not action, it's sitting! You deserve someone willing to act on your behalf, even in small ways, to show you they care and adore you. You should prefer the one who is willing to jump fences for you rather than sit on fences for you! That's adoration. Do not be impressed by the one who can "get any girl," be impressed with the one who has the integrity to be faithful to the one special girl and maybe one day have the courage to put a ring on her finger and promise to satisfy her every day for the rest of her life. That's adoration.

To adore takes initiative. He doesn't need a special day to adore you, he can take the initiative to adore you any day of the week because you deserve it. His admiration of you causes him to initiate special dates, gifts, occasions, and moments because he adores you and adoration demands initiative. It doesn't have to be your birthday, Valentine's Day, or a holiday to celebrate you. To adore you means that he takes the initiative to make any day *your* day because it's you and your love that make it special. And just like a compass without a needle is not a compass, a man without initiative is not a man.

To adore you is to love so dearly that the words "I love you," although appreciated, are not needed because his actions already clearly validate his adoration.

R

RESPECT ME

re·spect   noun /ri-ˈspekt/

- a feeling of admiring someone or something that is good, valuable, important, etc.

Mother Theresa once said that the worst poverty is the poverty of abandonment. I can surmise such abandonment is so severe because abandonment is the ultimate disrespect. To be devalued, discounted, marginalized, and ultimately deemed that you simply do not count so deeply scars the heart that the resuscitation of hope is rare and often unlikely. Who can bear the weight of being viewed as unimportant? You deserve **respect**.

Your personhood is priceless. Anyone committed to care for you or bold enough to pledge his love to you will without question respect you. He will respect your need to at times have your own space. He will respect your need to have an audience of one who willingly listens to the trials and triumphs of your day regardless of how seemingly trite or tremendous they may be. He will respect the fact that people come in all shapes and sizes, and it is not his place to push you into his ideal but accept you as you are because you are the miracle of life. He will respect your emotions because your emotions are you. He will respect your passions because they make your heart beat a rhythm he wants to learn and love. He will respect your wishes for they are snapshots of your dreams. He will respect your interests because their diversity paints a picture of the beauty of you that no one sees. He will respect your tears because he will want to know one day how to ease your pain and learn how to turn your frowns to smiles.

If he disrespects himself, disrespecting you will be easy. If he's smoking, he's disrespecting his body. If he compromises with alcohol and drugs, he is disrespecting his life. If he is indifferent about his life plan and purpose, he disrespects his Creator. Self-destructive behavior disrespects not only oneself but sets one's relationship up for catastrophe. Don't look the other way when you see him disrespecting himself or others, your turn is coming. It may not be today or tomorrow, but disrespect breeds disrespect. Respect is the only option.

You are important. You matter! Demand it. To accept anything less speaks more of you than of him. If you tolerate his disrespect, abuse is inevitable. Be mindful to respect yourself. You lose credibility with your expectations of him when you fail to respect yourself, either by your own actions or the disrespect you endure but say absolutely nothing about. It's not the fruit that falls at your feet that's most valuable, it's the fruit you have to reach for!

Be the fruit he has to reach for...not the fruit that falls at his feet.

G.E.

GOD'S EXPRESSION

God   noun /gäd/

- (in Christianity and other monotheistic religions) the creator and ruler of the universe and source of all moral authority; the supreme being.

ex·pre·ssion   noun /ik'spre SHən/

- the process of making known one's thoughts or feelings

The miracle of life is one of humankind's all-time greatest mysteries. It is too remarkable simply to leave to chance or coincidence. As one of the world's most renowned brain surgeons Dr. Ben Carson once said, "I don't have that much faith to believe the perfect human design is the result of one random evolutionary cell."

The gift of life is too astonishingly complex to assume there can be no designer, originator, or creator God. He formed you and fashioned you in your mother's womb, and He knew you at your conception. Out of your father's 250 million swimming candidates that were eligible to fertilize the egg, God chose you. About eighteen days later your heart beat for the very first time. It beat another 54 million times before you were born and will beat another 3.2 billion times throughout your lifetime.

You are nothing short of a miracle. You are fearfully and wonderfully made, complete with a unique personality, skill set, fingerprint, DNA, purpose, and destiny.

Scientists continue to be amazed at the uniqueness of each of the 7 billion people currently on Earth and the estimated 108 billion people who have ever lived. No two were ever completely alike.

You are God's Expression.

Your smile is unique, as are your glance, your eyes, your laugh, your notions and emotions. They are all distinctly you. You were called into existence for a reason and a purpose. To your Creator's delight, you are who you are. And if someone directs you or expects you to act like or be like someone you are not, they are asking you to live your life as a counterfeit, forfeiting your identity. No matter how you arrived and regardless of the circumstances of your birth, anticipated or not, the Great Designer designed you as you are, and He gave you life. The simple unmistakable fact that you are here is proof of that.

The canvas of your life is a masterpiece upon which you continue to create every day. Your daily experiences and the life lessons derived all craft beautiful you. It is not to say that the road you travel will be without mistakes or heartache. If enlightenment comes from those times that you've intentionally or unintentionally displayed a lapse in judgment, maybe the next time that there are two paths to choose you will have gained the wisdom to take the high road and have the courage to choose it each time thereafter. As one great leader said, sometimes you win, sometimes you learn.

You are God's Expression.

In a more practical sense, this affirmation should be understood first when defining Charge. For because you are God's Expression, you deserve to be Cherished, Honored, Adored and Respected.

This is the C.H.A.R.G.E.!

If he cannot respect the Charge, kindly ask him to sit down so you can see the one who will…because… he's simply not the one.

DECLARATION

I, _____ , understand the meaning of
C.H.A.R.G.E. So, from this day forward
C.H.A.R.G.E. will be my standard. When
choosing with whom to spend my time, I can now
identify the behaviors I should expect, as well as
what I should reject. I am unique. I am one of a
kind. I am and forever will be an original. I
deserve to be **Cherished, Honored, Adored, and
Respected**. I am **God's Expression**. I will not
rush. I will be patient. I will resist pressure to
move quickly.

Love is always patient, always kind. If he is
in a hurry, he may not be the one for me. I can
accept that. My todays will be brighter for this.
My tomorrows will be better for this. I will not
ignore any red flag I detect in his words, actions,
or associations. Just as a seatbelt protects my life
in a moving vehicle, wisdom to respond
appropriately to red flags protects my heart. I will
not compromise these values. I know in my life
pain and suffering may happen, but misery is an
option.

Love… shouldn't… hurt!

ABOUT THE AUTHOR

Steve Fitzhugh is a champion for youth, motivator, author, and humorist gifted at reaching all audiences! Because of his unique communication skills and effective presentation style, Mr. Fitzhugh remains in high demand. If your next event calls for a high energy, engaging, passionate, and effective messenger for any demographic of youth, consider Steve Fitzhugh and PowerMoves to make your event memorable and life-changing!

www.PowerMoves.org

www.ingramcontent.com/pod-product-compliance
Lightning Source LLC
Chambersburg PA
CBHW071801020426
42331CB00008B/2363